LOST ALPHABET
LISA OLSTEIN

COPPER CANYON PRESS
PORT TOWNSEND, WASHINGTON

Cover art: Rosamond Purcell, *Moths and music,* 1989. Collage of termite-eaten music and moths.

Copper Canyon Press is in residence at Fort Worden State Park in Port Townsend, Washington, under the auspices of Centrum. Centrum is a gathering place for artists and creative thinkers from around the world, students of all ages and backgrounds, and audiences seeking extraordinary cultural enrichment.

Grateful acknowledgment is made to the editors of *Fairy Tale Review, Forklift Ohio, jubilat,* the Manila Broadsides, Notnostrums.com, *Orion,* and PoetrySky.com, where some of these poems first appeared; and to the Massachusetts Cultural Council and Centrum.

For their invaluable encouragement and keen observations during the writing of this book, I thank Dara, Rob, Christian, Michelle, Noy, Kris, and David. For their enduring support, I thank my family and friends.

LIBRARY OF CONGRESS CATALOGING-IN-PUBLICATION DATA
Olstein, Lisa, 1972–
  Lost alphabet / Lisa Olstein.
    p. cm.
ISBN 978-1-55659-301-7 (alk. paper)
1. Entomologists—Poetry. 2. Moths—Poetry.
3. Metamorphosis—Poetry. I. Title.

PS3615.L78L67 2009
811'.6—dc22

2008053486

98765432 first printing

COPPER CANYON PRESS
Post Office Box 271
Port Townsend, Washington 98368
www.coppercanyonpress.org

FOR TOBY

CONTENTS

*

*

On starting a journey, do not turn back.

[my only life]

I have arrived in a place I think I will stay for a while. My shadow is cast before me by the paleness of a certain star after the moon is down. It won't last long—another week, maybe two. It's like nothing I've seen. Night floats through watery light. People step out at a certain hour. At first I didn't know why, then I joined them.

[sometimes they worship fire]

The people here know nothing they will reveal in my presence. I watch wrists and doorways, guess at the jewelry passed from mother to son. Near the river, all the boards lie easterly; near the place they gather, to the north. They have thrown me several parties: homemade whiskey and dancing, music played with a dull spoon on the side of a pig. There is a saying: No bad news at night. Save it for morning, or never.

[dreamy little savage]

Light is a blanket or a basin in which to wash. Then it is
nothing again, and here I am, there the plains, the well, the
watering hole, animals congregated there, a herd of low
clouds on the horizon. The last healer I went to was haughty
and would not look me in the eye. The gesture for come here
looks like go away. No is said with the flick of an eyebrow,
a soft click of the tongue.

[white spring]

I am working on a specimen so pale it is like staring at snow
from the bow of a ship in fog. I lose track of things—
articulation of wing, fineness of hair—as if the moth itself
disappears but remains as an emptiness before me. Or, from
its bleakness, the subtlest distinctions suddenly increase: the
slightest shade lighter in white begins to breathe with a
starkness that's arresting, and the very idea of color terrifies.
It has snowed and the evening is blue. The herders look like
buoys, like waders the water has gotten too deep around.
They'll have to swim in to shore. Their horses are patient.
They love to be led from their stalls. They love to sharpen
their teeth on the gate. They will stand, knees locked, for
hours.

[the small brain is very old]

I am running nighttime experiments: a white sheet strung between posts, illuminated with moonlight and coned torches. If the moon is what guides them, light is never meant to be close, but a far beacon by which to steer. Nearer brightness is a mistake—they are unprepared. Some species visit soon after dusk; some don't arrive until nearly dawn. Some swing directly toward the appearance of light, hit the sheet with their wings, cling there. Others approach the luminescence, but keep a certain distance. Not every species goes for the torch when I remove its cover, but most do. The space at the center of the flame fools them; they turn and seek the middle darkness.

[for a moment I was cured]

I woke again today with the steel helmet tightening. Dreams wander. Pain arrives at first like chance, as if it just so happened, as if it were required of a situation, like fear in a fight. It is best if I sit up quickly, but I rarely sit up quickly, usually too late and the helmet is in place. Light is blinding. I must not lean back or even raise my feet to a stool. I'm glad for visitors when they come. Now that the villagers know of my work they bring me pictures. They see the moths as compositions of color and line, and assume I might study theirs as well.

[if you are here you have already come too far]

Perhaps I stay because they are a horse people and I miss my stable. I've arranged with a local trader to visit his stalls. With the animals, the scrim of language is pulled back and I am fluent. With men, it may be easier without words— certain arguments never arise. I find myself caring for people I know almost nothing about except the way they move their eyes across my face, their eyes across their fields, how likely they are to put a hand on my shoulder, to laugh or slap a horse when thrown.

[species at rest]

I've decided where I will hide if thieves come, and, if found, what I'll reveal of my possessions, in what order. There's not much here but the moths in their envelopes, notebooks, drawings. Certain utensils are difficult to find and I would not give them up without a fight. It's surprising, how the currency of a place might be in wooden spoons, iron pots, how quickly we believe it.

[wings are folded in a myriad of ways]

During the cold months they keep miniature gardens in their homes, tiny plots of seedlings and herbs. Rosemary looks like giant cypress. I see them gaze longingly at the animals in their pens as if wishing a goat might shrink to size. They eye my moths—what beautiful birds to inhabit their landscapes if only they would come alive and stay.

[kindred forms]

When not studying specimens, I see their features everywhere: fine-rivered hair on a baby's head, bright cloth he's bundled in, angle of a lamb's ear. Then, at the examination table, the world presses in: dusk on the forewing, crenellations of castles at the tip, antennae like the jaws of fossil fish pressed into the riverbed. It is remarkable to be far from any coast and still to feel at the very tip of land, the last place.

[no luck at all]

They have no word for it or refuse to and believe wind itself carries what comes—dust of drought, dust of storm, dust of calm. When it is very still they believe time has stopped for as long as nothing moves across the face. Belief itself is convincing: fields lie frozen, animals quiet in their pens, and the only sound is the low ticking of vegetables underground. My friend Ilya says you have no friend Ilya, says you have to envy the whole life.

[all the idolaters in the world]

I am gaining a reputation. Before, not much attention
was paid. Now village traders bring specimens to me upon
their return. Suddenly, pulled from pockets or little tents
of sackcloth arrive sphinxes and sackbearers, owlets,
clearwings, mimics. I thank the men in their custom: a meal
prepared and all but the smallest portions laid by a rock at
the edge of town. It is not that they think the stone is
hungry—it's an occasion for animals to come and eat.

[but new snow is forever falling on the old]

It is customary to pray for sound health and good understanding. Ilya says to be more specific is unwise—it's a mistake to believe we know what we require. We are guided in directions we don't know how to imagine. God is generous in not making us appear foolish every time. We move forward as if in a blizzard, building cairns from the bones of our horses to serve as landmarks in the snow, and later, to remind us of something when we look across the blazing plain.

[the heart is always behind the fingers]

Each specimen is brought into position with the stroke of a small feather. This to keep the powders undisturbed, each color in its place. Nevertheless, I am clumsy. Today I made the mistake of attempting to scrape from a lappet's forewing what appeared to be a murky residue before realizing it was the wing itself. Possible camouflage markings for a swamp life.

[receding sphinx]

I'm working with a common family of flower feeders. Many
are wide-ranging and have already been identified: one-eyed,
laurel, waved, walnut, lettered. I have found one, however, I
believe to be new to classification. Its wings have the rippled
driftwood of a modest and the hot crimson of a twin
spotted. In shape and size, the body is what you would
expect: short, round, tapered at the tip, but here the
similarities end. The whole trunk appears to be clear like the
transparent wings of a hummingbird or wasp mimic. In the
case of a lucent wing, we see through the veined panels to
whatever happens to be on the other side, but this is like
peering through glass into some unpupiled eye.

[had I time had I power]

One day out requires three days in. The balance used to be reversed. I am loath to move from one notebook to the next, from one specimen to another. Surely important things are missed. I want nothing to end, not a single observation, despite longing for what remains unknown. For one thing: weight. Another: ratio. Flight's beat, beat, glide. And constantly, the interruption: sometimes circling for days, a wary insistent stray. Ilya sees it before I do, on my face, one side sagging, a pulled shade. I see the seeing, wait for the pain to descend, distantly, as if this sorrow were not mine.

[if it ever happens that the fire goes out]

Someone I love has died. I am certain, but I cannot tell who. A bird that sounds like a cuckoo calls the hours like an old clock, only not the hours we mean. I think I see into each day, but it is every thing in its turn reflecting the sky, tossing back what it is shown. Through the window, an owl announces tonight's neatly wrapped package of bone and fur. There is no rope swing unraveling in the moonlight. You cannot hope backwards or in reverse.

*

The invisible is not a negation or a contradiction of the visible
but simply its secret sharer.

[the dark one with the seed in its beak]

There's nothing to do for the cold. I haul what burns. It's not hard to remember summer's heat, the feeling is much the same: everything swathed in temperature, burning. I broke a glass in the hut and have not swept it up. I walk at night pretending I can sense where to put my foot down. If there are unnecessary words, what are they? This morning all the crows returned as one darkly shimmering field. Now they rise and resettle on the winterweed, green with its diet of snow.

[tearful underwing]

When I have been away from the table too long it is difficult to begin. There is a thrill, then a calm, then despair. When there is no satisfaction in the work, in not working and walking through the fields, I follow the river in my mind, south by southwest, back the way I came. Someone has tied a flag to the wind. It flaps a steady drum: north north. When I am not myself, Ilya tries to remind me. This, I did not foresee.

[no camouflage requires decoration like this]

Having gone so deeply into the maze of dung- and dust-colored, the brightly painted come as a shock. Saturation of pigment brings a uniformity to their extravagance the modest shades don't require. At first they seem obvious, savage in their displays, but no colors are incongruous in nature. Here, the effect of study is not entry but being entered. Fields of hot color pulse outward. The eye—finger of the soul—responds with varying degrees of constriction, expansion, extending backwards to the brain. In the field, I have observed birds capture and release day-flying crimsons from their beaks. There are only a few I can't bear to study.

[saturniidae]

It would be impossible to choose among them: jeweled eyes disperse the gaze. Up close, they dilate, they open like mouths across a green field of wing. The lower trunk shimmers with secret intentions; it hides behind a white cloak. There is a red river coming. There is a bend. The true eyes pool behind a hood of pale feathers. It is mesmerizing, unlike any camouflage I have ever seen. The limitations are those of my imagination.

[a raven touched his eyebrow]

Ilya sits with me through the morning and into the afternoon—scapegoat, savior, nursemaid, fool—brings drink I cannot drink. Slowly, the absence of pain arrives like snow falling. It was on a day like this when, visiting, Ilya decided to stay. At least, never left. It is customary here to accompany the wounded. Whoever is able, and near.

[from this you will wish to make romance]

This moment could be any moment since the moment I
arrived. The fields are made of ice. The ice could be the
river's mercury vapors, its languid meniscus lip. Wind
stitches current. It could easily be north. One day last week
I thought I saw a child's balloon, but it was a bird sitting on
the neck of a girl. Now I see them everywhere. He nips his
beak back and forth, runs his black tongue against her ear.
Even when he is completely still it's as if she is directed: time
to walk quickly, time to speak softly, time for fingers, no
fingers ruffling his crest.

[unsated beauty]

I have run out of thread and everything here is sewn with horsehair made fine by running it through the teeth. So this is what I use to mend my clothes and to close the specimens after dissection. They say it is cleaner than our own spit. At first I was careful to soak it in well water before bringing it to my lips; now I sit and pull strands back and forth as absently as any herder.

[since deaths are frequent they are never done
with mourning]

They know how long the dead should hover and when one
has hovered too long. There are practices for this situation.
Nothing is required of the grieving. Silently the village takes
up around them, passing their custody from one to another,
so that someone is always there braiding horsehair and
leather across the door. Yesterday, either from shame of
paucity or wishful thinking, I told a gathering of men that,
where I'm from, when a loved one dies we cut our thumbs
and pace our fields letting drops of blood rose a path. Ilya
watched me with the same look as when I state as fact
something about the moths that is merely hypothesis.

[the miraculous paradox]

Sometimes, once opened, everything in the body moves forward. There's no predicting this and nothing to be done except to let the contents spill or to quickly cinch the cut with pins. In some cases, the pressure subsides. Sometimes, it's as if some force, once risen, must continue to rise.

[I met him on his island]

People come here and their hair grows long. Travelers and
traders arrive clean, men willing to shave on the back of a
horse, and here they stop. Ilya says our dark universe is
really the belly of some beast. If in the beginning I revered in
Ilya some native wisdom, this is no longer true. Lately, I look
at Ilya with the contempt reserved for those who remind us
of our former selves. Ilya looks at me as if only a monster or
a fool.

[master thunder]

A fierce wind blows the wrong birds to the fields, as if to a distant shore. They land dazed, a hundred, more, near to one another, making no sound. Women set out pans of warm mash as they do for early foals. I used to tell them when they asked about the things and places I've seen. I remember less and less. Who am I here in this village? Who am I anywhere? In the morning they'll charge the fields with brooms to help the birds on their way.

[the immovable moves]

I have learned to peer at specimens through a small crack at
the center of my fist. It's a habit herders use for distance:
vision is concentrated, the crude tunnel brings into focus
whatever small expanse lies on the other side, something in
the narrowing magnifies what remains. At the table, my hand
tires of clenching, my left eye of closing, my right of its
squint, but the effect: a blurred carpet of wing becomes a
careful weave of eyelashes colored, curved, exquisitely laid. It
is a lens for looking at fractions; I'm unable to bring even a
whole antenna or eye into view. The result is kaleidoscopic: I
see one sharp fragment after another break clean before me,
piece it to the others in my mind's eye.

[the usual dead]

I wake at the wrong hours. Night showers arrive abruptly, lay down their music swiftly, no soft murmuring to appease. One needs very little light to see by. Hard darkness where the eyes widen blankly is difficult to find, impossible to manufacture. The senses shift. Let go from the head, they fill the arms and the fingers, though they are still, fill the torso, though it quivers. I perceive currents otherwise untended, as when on horseback with eyes closed, it is effortless to follow the reach and pull, to feel every jump as it gathers. I am only the rider.

[myriad myriad forms]

My eyes have adjusted to looking more and more closely.
Color separates each hour. What from a distance seems a
continuous plane becomes a sea of dappled islands, broken,
a softness of shards. I distinguish brims of fountain basins
from the water's lapping edge, figures clothed in pine woods
at dusk. A bird I remember from my childhood is standing
in the road. It enters the mirage to drink, then returns to the
dusty river.

[unsated sallow]

What appears smooth is feathered. What appears feathered is scaled. They are armored in perfect chain mail. Disciplined soldiers, the plates are strictly aligned no matter how riotous the pattern. Orderly farmers, neat rows span the field in straight lines. Every row a column of small squares of exact proportion. They open inward, as if each one contains a larger space inside.

[each river was a river of mercury]

Am I meant simply to observe, to record? How will I know when this work is done? There are things to which I mean to be true. I'm no longer sure what they are, but I recognize falsity's tin ring. I search and it finds me. I move, it moves, too. What discovery will lead me from who I am? If I could wake as a blank field, a cloud-covered plain, wind in the place of each memory, what would I choose?

[any such bold claim]

We are ringed by hills. I've taken to burying almost anything
that dies—spiders, mice, birds I find in the road. This goes
against local custom; here they burn. I question what I eat.
How death makes it possible, but not dead long. Not too
newly, either. There is no beauty in this, which is what draws
me. I expect certain things to correct themselves, but sheep
remain dumb in bickering light. Whatever part of this can be
gotten rid of, I want gone. Whatever part must be taken,
taken inside.

*

The more you know, the more beautiful everything is.

[a new typology]

I can no longer stand the dead in their colorful rows. I spend all day circling around myself. Why this constant pursuit? We're embarrassed by reality, the things that are crushing out of sweetness. Through the classifications I can see something happening. I'm trying to render the sun with the good draftsmanship of a child. There is a victory every minute. It will never be more exalted.

[root entry]

Lines mark them as if palms to be read, but animate—like
veins, they suggest deep movement, a flowing under ground,
busy corridors. I have no evidence that anything moves
through them. In the past when I cut, wings disassembled:
stained-glass panels along lead frames. This among the dead,
so of course nothing moved. Any cut to the living seems to
bring about a freezing: nothing to be gained. I learn more by
hovering my fingers above their dark channels, but it
remains difficult to trust this knowledge or to give it a name.

[order and system]

I'm beginning to understand. They say thunder and lightning are dragon, not symbol or sign but body and bone and breath and sigh. They say the sun is a revelation. The blue sky. I'm ashamed of how I feel, constantly wasteful, but I don't know what I spend. I grow uglier all the time. Ilya says the invisible is neither ugly nor beautiful. The moths say nothing. I didn't mean to be so hungry, as if they exist for my comprehension alone.

[newcomers to the field of endeavor]

There's something dead in the road. No one will touch it. The specimen I'm studying won't sit still. I can no longer do it: swab the ether, drop it into the flapping jar. Ilya watches me from across the room. If I lay the jar on its side with the lid removed eventually the moth will slow its beating. A rinse of sugar-water at the rim draws it to the edge, keeps it there drinking, for a moment, as if from a great glass flower. I usually have time to record family and size, primary markings. This one moves quickly, lights for barely a second at a time. Soon it will fly off and come to rest on some other surface in the room, usually the rough ceiling, which is becoming winged with them.

[a lesson in liberty]

And then Ilya storms and then Ilya is sullen. Then Ilya wants
it wordlessly forgiven and I do. What have we become to
each other that accounts for this? In the village the men are
changing houses; the women are staying put. It is some kind
of anniversary. I ask what is commemorated. Ilya says your
face is ugly tonight, turn the page.

[the second of five predictables]

It is injurious to move them, no matter how gently, from whatever perch or bed they are quiet upon. Anything hates to be pulled from its feet. They resist and soon it's a struggle and I'm some monster of weather or prey, so I have learned to move them carefully on whatever it is they cling to. There is a ripple, an almost undetectable flash of alarm, but it passes, and the branch or leaf beneath them is a balm, a promise between us.

[immaculate holomelina]

Birds sew leaves together with dead blades of grass. A fog rises from the blank fields as if they exhale now that the stingy early crops are finally gone. Any suggestion of storm sends a shimmer through the hut, but this seems to calm them. Perhaps the fog leadens their wings; perhaps the milky landscape is like blindness or sleep. Today's specimen sits completely still. Red forewing. Red hindwing. Red trunk. Red eyes.

[the uppermost is fire]

My legs fill with smoke. Jagged stones rattle and grind. I'm restless until stilled, dumb and unsound, a body of contradictions: I love almost anything, can stand to be near very little. I go numb. I am sensitive to the gentlest movement of air. I'm reckless. I'm fearful, nervous even of the tame village strays. I talk too much, too loudly, unable to find the simplest words.

[so much for this city]

I seem to emerge from each bout with new ideas about the moths. I'm not aware of contemplating them during the pain, but when I return to the table some sort of transformation occurs. It's not scientific, but in the way I see them or realize that I don't. If I keep my face impassive, they are more likely to turn to me. They seem to say what has appeared useful to you is of no use. These are not the ones I bungled with early hands. These I harm in ways I don't know yet, but can be sure of.

[both the specific remedy and the condition
of health]

Some mornings I'm filled with longing, with sadness that has
no cause. It alights when we are busy or when we are still, as
often on the heels of success as of failure. No matter the
weather, which no longer affects me as once it did. In wanting
to show the best of myself, I reveal only a fraction. There is
a swimming, a gasping for air. Even the presence of the
moths, what they suggest, is crowding. Their silence grows.

[if the cities are not given]

I keep handling to a minimum. Fingers are too blunt. Because the way I touch them decides everything—if they'll sit still—I practice using string and dead specimens from the drawers: slip a length beneath the wings, hold it out on either side, flip the body, gently, like wind. When done smoothly, they appear animate again, only mesmerized, lying perfectly still, legs and abdomen exposed.

[it is dangerous to love what death can touch]

Even within a single family, size and shape can be so varied the only way I know for sure what I study is to raise them. Otherwise I might think I'm looking at five or six different species when really it is one. There is a certain caterpillar whose camouflage is half worm, half ant, so each specimen appears to be both predated and predator—perpetual carrion perpetually being dragged off.

[at first it is less than a grain of millet]

They are as strict in their habits as the moths they become.
We guess at their needs and hope to do no harm. The first
hours and days are a grave concern. Nocturnals hatched in
morning wander all day over leaves and branches that as
soon as darkness falls they devour: night feeders. Some
emerge from their casings and never look back. Others
linger near as if to a good home before venturing forth.
Certain species take their first meal from this incubator shell:
skin eaters. If removed, they will eat nothing and die.

[instar]

Each specimen is scented. It's difficult to believe I was so
unaware. Sometimes fragrance rings from a single caterpillar;
sometimes it is undetectable until much later, wafting from a
flock of like wings. Tins of dust and fine sand suit most
varieties. As long as there is food they seem not to notice one
another. They rest alone or touching. At regular intervals
they undergo surges in growth that seem to require the
shedding of their skin, but this we have not been able to
document. We observe a distinct quieting of activity, a
settling on a small white pillow of excrement several hours in
the making. There is almost nothing to see. Slowly they seem
to swell from turning inward. They draw in their borders,
press out again larger, imperfectly known.

[the blessing you hope never to come near]

Morning. Nothing suits me—fine lamplit wind under the brighter lights of dawn. No matter what I learn, there are reversions. I rely on silence, but I'm desperate to speak, to be spoken to. Sometimes a consciousness sifts up as if everything that's happened never happened at all, wonders where are my schedules, my tidy specimen drawers? For the most part, though, change strikes like a whipping cord—once is enough.

[an analogy is enough]

The waiting is interminable. A cocoon thins and colors. Where it was brown and leaflike, it becomes fog on glass disappearing. A vein shines through, pulses. For days I think I see movement where there is no movement. Then, a trembling barely distinguishable from my own breath. The opening is unlikely as a magician's sleight of hand: you should not believe but do. Common boundaries no longer guide you. There is an unfolding as if of a lady's fan. Three have hatched in the predawn. Ilya sleeps in bed. They sit trembling near the papery husks they inhabited—wobbly ships on a river of ships.

*

These are the soul's changes.

[a moment or as long as necessary]

Like captains on a ship or cousins in a poorhouse we sleep in
shifts, one of us always watching. Ilya won't handle the
specimens, but reports their activity in a log. Usually days are
quiet. I have imagined a new way of holding my instruments,
more of a laying down in the fingers. I introduce the changes
slowly so as not to startle the moths. It will benefit them, but
they are accustomed to what they are accustomed to and I
don't want them to think I am strange.

[celestial bodies]

At dusk men spread out through the village, the fields,
taking up positions unmarked. For three nights this is
where they spend the night, in pairs, wrapped in dark
clothes. It is as if they shelter in invisible structures,
monitoring carefully chosen lookout posts. The moon is
bright upon them, at each station, one kneeling, one lying
on the ground. I can't read any logic in their arrangements.
Ilya says watch. Patterns emerge. Finally, I see it: they creep
like constellations across the sky.

[dark lanterns]

We have learned to move silently in the daytime. It is
essential that the moths get their rest. If we stumble about
unthinkingly, their sleep breaks open in the light. Confusion
sets in; they won't eat, they won't stop flying. Weeks of early
deaths demonstrated the exquisite equation by which they
survive. Interrupt their sleep and hours are used out of turn.
There will be a price to pay. If our work rouses one, we have
no choice but to pin it before the rest make up their minds
to fly.

[oak beauty]

Placid for days, no movement, no marked change, then in the final moments a jerking confusion. We watch it struggle, as if clamoring to stay in or get out, as if in death throes flickering. It is a commotion, an event, this emergence, violence waked from sleep then slowed again to something lovely, unlike death when it does come, which comes softly, a slow exhalation.

[a twilight figure]

A chance freeze has belled the fence posts, glassed the grass
into a still museum. Ordinarily we gather leaves each
morning to feed the caterpillars; this morning there's
nothing to do but shred notebook pages into their
enclosures. It is a critical juncture: what they eat now will
sustain their transformation and, later, their flying. The
fledglings also are in danger; if the moisture on their
unfolding wings freezes, there will be no remedy—to breathe
on them is a temptation but would only compound the
problem. We cover the window to darken the room. Ilya
walks in wide circles carrying a tray of lit candles. Slowly,
the moths begin to stir and follow.

[the universe within]

My mind shifts from thought to thought, unable to quiet. I never know, when this happens, what the cause. Soon, the pain may come, explain anything. I admit to being lonely. I think the river is watching me. I know the moths are watching it, with their antennae, their wings. They know it through the leaves they eat, their moisture and must. Sometimes there are voices. Sometimes sparks of light. These are always followed. The less defined—vagueness, wanderings—may not be. Laughter is a sure sign. Tears, not necessarily. I'm never lonely anymore.

[arrivals]

Moths ride the room as if a meadow. As if rainfall, hover, nectar, soar. I close my eyes. I feel them, the smell of them, the smell of me. Surely this insight is a defect. I will not cherish the pain or need it. As if to covet any part would render increase when it is clear that wishing is nothing. But there are patterns; parts of my brain gain voice, grow louder. Small doors of perception open, close.

[from this vantage point your view will be clear]

Any shift in philosophy introduces the need for new habits of
body. I am learning how gently to lift them, to turn them
swiftly and rest them again, on their wings, wings to table,
which I sand smooth each morning. To do it with no
fluttering, with as little as possible. It is a strange gymnastics,
their bodies, mine: what to grasp, when to release, the nature
of a turn, the will of the whole channeled into the fingertips.
It takes all my strength. It is necessary to practice, to imagine
myself the moth, my arms its wings, my legs gone.

[some superior heaven]

Small crowds in the distance. It is the same for emergency as for celebration: clots of bodies gathering and dispersing. A boy lies dead in a field. I don't know what killed him. I know his face, his habit of walking. We never spoke, but this was not unfriendly. He was found and his family was brought. One by one they move into the field and lie beside him. He will never enter their home again.

[when the consolations grow too few]

One has emerged with insufficient wing. We cannot know if
the defect was inevitable or born of some misfortune. Wing
drying is precarious: if in the first minute each is not
properly unfurled, there is no possibility of repair. In this
instance, the left fore is pinned back, a folded page. It will
never fly. I noticed it on the floor where it must have fallen
trying. It no longer tries. I offer the cripple-wing my finger.
She drinks sugar-water we set in puddles on a stool. Ilya
works to devise a reservoir to place at the heart of a flower,
one never-ending supply.

[those who have eyes to see]

This morning a trader woke us with knocking at the door.
A surprise. No one comes anymore. He has been away; he
is just returned. He brings with him from the east a small
box hung with string around his neck: two moths quite
alive. I am filled with trepidation. We don't know what they
require. It has been too long since we began blind, placing
one kind of leaf before a mute specimen, another. In the
beginning I thought the moths were without notice or
concern, but I have long recognized kindness in the way
they fly.

[the million]

Ordinarily there is very little flying: the hut is treated like the
rough trunk of an enormous tree. But for two nights the air
has hummed with them skipping and hovering. The first we
barely moved. The second we walked among them, wings
brushing our faces. They are not wild any longer, not tame.
In the bluing light they settle in twos, swaying slightly, as if
far beneath a lapping surface. We sit useless, watching. We
marvel at the immensity of their landscape. The hut is an
echo chamber, every surface whispering. It is an exhaustive
vigil. Pairs stay clasped together for hours.

[a path we long have known]

Needs arise: to remember, to insist, to forget. The moths' are straightforward: some things can be looked for, and if unfound done without; without some things, they die. Ilya tends to Ilya's alone, lately disappearing from the hut for an hour or two, a day. Once this might have thrilled me or done me harm. Now I let it. It lets me. In the quiet, we are fine.

*

I will not let thee go, except thou bless me.

[ghost moth]

The wind wakes them; they wake me. Like a lost alphabet, they await decipherment. I read in them what I desire, what I bring to the silence like a meal. There is hunger and then I am fed and soon I'm hungry again. I feel it in my body, there is a pulling in of bone, across my skin, it glows.

[partridges are plentiful and very cheap]

Their scent echoes what food we gather: sweetgrass in
spring, lavender when lavender blooms. These days, sun.
Birds bathe in dust for coolness, lie awkwardly on one side,
the other, drift it in small gray clouds across their backs.
Grasshoppers appear suddenly in the fields, springing up like
fountains. They sing, but not as loudly as I imagined—a
factor of the air, its power to disperse or concentrate. Song
is muted but the sound of jaws working is everywhere.

[species rich but little known]

I spread brews of rotten fruit on trees, on the side of the hut, in the dark. Some species will pierce the skin of fruit or animal with hollow tongues. I lead sleeping sheep from their pens. Some do not eat at all, subsisting all their winged life on what reserves they built before. I stop taking notes. Some resemble bird droppings. There is too much to quantify, to pretend can be quantified. Some are flightless. I don't know what purpose this serves. I am beginning to understand seeing itself as the endeavor—an activity of the eye, over when it is closed.

[flowerdeep]

Something in Ilya is receding. I cannot keep my mind on it
for long. There is too much activity. The plain is rising;
across it, horse meadows come into bloom. The fields have
so many million parts. Moths move through the air like fish
in the river. All waters everywhere in concert.

[whites and sulphurs]

We wake in snowlight from horizon to horizon. It is not
snow but smoke drifting slowly in. Every shift in current
changes the way it reaches us—low gray pillows that turn
the sun red, high and white, fine as mist off the river. The
horses' eyes burn. At least, they weep before our own, which
soon weep. They behave as usual. The fires are far off. Men
gather in the road, tell stories of animals turning back into
the burning stalls from which they were just released.

[the fullness of his powers]

My second skin is beginning to feel like a second skin. It comes in clusters, bundling light into shadow and piercing brightness. In the dull part of the afternoon when the village is dusty with sleep. A hawk taunts a dog. I sit by the window, face wrapped in cloth. Flowers press closed heat-stroked petals: moth sticks, pinwheel stills. I can smell Ilya's breath from across the room, vegetables that passed by in someone's arms. I feel everything just before it arrives.

[when hunger is sure to be present]

Today a ragged column of men returned. I had not known
any were missing, had not heard absent sons or lovers
mentioned by anyone. They are not very many, but enough.
To fill a wagon, to harvest a field. From the hut I watch them
walk by. No one comes out to greet them. Doors shut.
Quietly, they are refused entrance to their village. Ilya says
yes, it is their village. Quietly, they leave.

[theory of clouds]

I am training myself to identify species solely by the sound of their wings. I sit blindfolded and one by one Ilya sets them flying. The papery whispers are remarkably easy to hear, but it is by the weight of their bodies—cloud hands—that I am learning to know them, when they land on me, as they are more and more apt to do.

[gossamer wings]

We move from the hut at dusk and dawn. We haul river water in reed buckets to refresh the cuttings on which everything depends. When it is too hot for this labor, we bring the leaves in baskets to the river and wade in with them, waist-high in the cooling. This morning, returning with our weeping parcels, we stepped into a hut of wilted flowers, everywhere wings loosening, failing like sails. I swab the walls with wet cloths. Those that have already fallen, Ilya paints with water from a fine horsehair brush.

[hawkweed and daisies]

An unexpected rain lets sweet from the plains. Horses kick
like it's spring for an hour, roll against the golden bristle
which is all that's left in the fields they've chewed down. The
heat of the day lasts in our hair, our clothes, in the wood of
the table. Ilya is meticulous, before bed sifting nail clippings
and hair into small cloth bags. Sometimes it is as if I work
all night to show in the morning what I have gathered.
Other times it is as if there is no one here at all.

[with this bridle to restrain them]

Now we use all of daylight for gathering seeds and stalks from the plants most favored by our moths, the ones we see them fly to through the darkness when we send them from the hut. We choose the gentlest hour. We send the strongest ones. We travel and re-travel the same ground. In the moonlight every body turns to silver. Some return—we think it is them—clinging to the hut at daybreak. They remain tame, our fingers able.

[the weather in here]

I have a plan to divert the river into this room, to provide the moths with the plants and reeds they desire. Ilya believes this is going too far and besides they won't be fooled. They will know our hut by the smell of us and wood, the feel of glass, even if we keep it wrapped. It is always wrapped now, but perhaps they will feel it through the cloth: a surface smoother than anything they require. Still, the air will be more hospitable and this is important—when I take down the window and the door, I want for them to stay.

[no one could count their number]

Through the pain I can hear someone speaking. Ilya with a
river cloth of reeds. Ilya who will not answer my questions.
There is a certain moth that appears always to be falling
away, even as it flies toward you. Rain is near. When it ends,
different moths will arrive in the fields. These last few nights
in the hut there has been a rustling. All those we kept from
leaving now ready themselves to return.

NOTES

On starting a journey, do not turn back. —Pythagoras

The invisible is not a negation or a contradiction of the visible but simply its secret sharer. —Lucien Taylor

The more you know, the more beautiful everything is. —George Santayana

These are the soul's changes. —Virginia Woolf

I will not let thee go, except thou bless me. —Genesis

For images, terminology, and occasional phrases that inspired this project, I'm indebted to *Night Visions: The Secret Designs of Moths,* by Joseph Scheer; *Fabre's Book of Insects,* illustrated by E.J. Detmold; *Audubon's Butterflies, Moths, and Other Studies,* edited by Alice Ford; *Moths and How to Rear Them,* by Paul Villiard; *Speak, Memory,* by Vladimir Nabokov; and *The Travels,* by Marco Polo.

ABOUT THE AUTHOR

Lisa Olstein is the author of *Radio Crackling, Radio Gone,* winner of the 2005 Hayden Carruth Award (Copper Canyon Press, 2006). *Cold Satellite,* an album of songs based on her writing, was released by singer-songwriter Jeffery Foucault in 2009. She is the recipient of a Pushcart Prize and fellowships from the Massachusetts Cultural Council and Centrum. A contributing editor of *jubilat,* with Dara Wier and Noy Holland she co-founded the Juniper Initiative for Literary Arts and Action at the University of Massachusetts Amherst, where she is associate director of the M.F.A. Program for Poets and Writers.

The Chinese character for poetry is made up of two parts: "word" and "temple." It also serves as pressmark for Copper Canyon Press.

Since 1972, Copper Canyon Press has fostered the work of emerging, established, and world-renowned poets for an expanding audience. The Press thrives with the generous patronage of readers, writers, booksellers, librarians, teachers, students, and funders—everyone who shares the belief that poetry is vital to language and living.

Major funding has been provided by:
Anonymous
Beroz Ferrell & The Point, LLC
Lannan Foundation
National Endowment for the Arts
Cynthia Lovelace Sears and Frank Buxton
Washington State Arts Commission

For information and catalogs:
COPPER CANYON PRESS
Post Office Box 271
Port Townsend, Washington 98368
360-385-4925
www.coppercanyonpress.org

The principal typeface for these poems is Sabon, an old-style serif typeface created by the German-born typographer and designer Jan Tschichold in the 1960s. Headings are set in Orator, created by John Scheppler in 1962 for IBM type-writers. Book design and composition by Phil Kovacevich. Printed at BookMobile.

LOST ALPHABET